This work is a tribute to Outward Bound instructors everywhere. With generosity and diligence, they share with others their respect and love for this planet and all its inhabitants.

Published by:
Beyond Words Publishing, Inc.
13950 NW Pumpkin Ridge Road
Hillsboro, Oregon USA 97123
Phone: 1-503-647-5109
Toll Free: 1-800-284-9673

Printed in Singapore

ISBN: 0-941831-64-7
Library of Congress Catalog Card Number: 91-71043

Cover and book design by Principia Graphica

For information on a slide presentation or video program of this book, please contact the publisher.

OUTWARD BOUND
THE
INWARD ODYSSEY

PHOTOGRAPHY
Mark Zelinski

TEXT EDITOR
Gary Shaeffer

"Outward Bound" is the meaning of the "Blue Peter" signal flag hoisted by merchant ships as they leave harbour for foreign ports. The combined experience and skills of the navigator, the seaman, and the engineer are needed to ensure that a ship makes a safe journey. Outward Bound was, therefore, an apt choice as the name for an organisation designed to help young men about to start their careers in the British Merchant Navy at the height of the Second World War. It is easy enough to teach technical skills; it is quite another matter to exercise those skills in the stress of Atlantic gales and in the face of submarine attacks.

Outward Bound had been the brainchild of Laurence Holt, of the Blue Funnel Line, and Kurt Hahn, the Headmaster of Gordonstoun School. I had been a pupil at Gordonstoun, so it came as no surprise to be invited to become the Patron of Outward Bound in 1953. Since that time I have had the opportunity to visit most of the schools and centres around the world.

It all began in a small way at Aberdovey in North Wales in 1941. The idea has since spread through 18 countries in 5 continents, and there is plenty of scope for further expansion. From the very beginning Outward Bound was intended to develop self-confidence and self-awareness through self-discovery. This is the "Inward Odyssey" of the title; it is what Carl Jung described as the process of "individuation". Every individual needs the inner capacity to cope with the vicissitudes of life; this could be said to involve using the art of a navigator to avoid hazards, the craft of a seaman to weather storms, and the skill of an engineer to maintain the will to go on. It is the philosophy of Outward Bound that it is never too early or too late for anyone to begin the journey of self-discovery.

It is always difficult to illustrate a process intended to influence the development of character and attitude, but I hope that the words and images in this book will help to convey an impression of the means by which Outward Bound has successfully achieved its objects during the last 50 years.

HRH PRINCE PHILIP

2

"To me Outward Bound's chief work is enrichment, helping people to have life and to have it more abundantly. Our courses are supposed to mature people, and no doubt they do, but more importantly they keep people young so that they retain their child's sense of wonder at themselves and at their world. Fundamentally Outward Bound is about love, love and appreciation of life, love of people, and love of the planet we are privileged to live on. People who really love life go exploring; they are outward bound on the oceans of their lives, even though physically they may go no farther than their own back yards. They do not hoard themselves, they spend themselves. And paradoxically, it is the spending that enriches them."

Canadian Asset Management

Box Twenty, Greenbank, Ontario, Canada L0C 1B0

Phone: (416) 985-3751

Dear Reader:

Life's significant lessons are often learned outside the formal educational setting. The experience gained from the Outward Bound programmes have had dramatically positive effects on personal growth and development. We are honoured to have played a small part in this book which commemorates fifty years of such a noble cause.

Taking on challenges and setting large goals stretches the abilities of humankind. A greater benefit is realised when an enhanced personal perspective teaches us how to deal with others and ourselves.

This book captures so many incredible Outward Bound moments from the best classrooms on our planet.

Noreen E. Calderbank, P. Eng.

PARTNER

Ron E. Beck, B. Math.

PARTNER

Sun Life Assurance Company of Canada

150 King Street West Toronto, Ontario, Canada M5H 1J9

Phone (416) 979-9966

Dear Reader:

Sun Life Assurance Company of Canada and its 10,000 people around the world are proud to have contributed to the publication of this volume.

The book shows, in a dramatic way, the many diverse, exciting, and intriguing activities of Outward Bound. Here we have a dynamic, visual account of how people, young and old, from all walks of life and economic strata, and of different ethnic origins and cultures, have worked hard to make their lives fuller, richer, and more giving. I congratulate the men and women of Outward Bound who devise and direct the imaginative programmes depicted here.

Sun Life is in the business of building better lives. Moreover, our donations programme assists the physical, mental, and cultural health of the communities in which we operate. Thus, we considered a financial grant toward the publication of this volume to be very appropriate for our Company. We hope our contribution will prove to be a valuable investment for the Outward Bound cause.

John D. McNeil

CHAIRMAN AND CHIEF EXECUTIVE OFFICER

Kurt Hahn

Kurt Hahn was a man of remarkable vision and relentless energy. During the 1940s the dynamic mix of several singular men resulted in the establishment of the Aberdovey Sailing School, the founding of the Outward Bound Trust, and Aberdovey's successful transition from sailing school to Outward Bound centre.

Kurt Hahn, the patriarch of Outward Bound, was German-born but a lifelong Anglophile. From an early period, convinced that the good in everyone could be awakened and developed by the right environment and teaching, he was drawn to theories of education. He drew up plans for a new kind of school, which was first realised in the Schloss Salem near Lake Constance, the ancestral home of Prince Max von Baden, Hahn's benefactor. Borrowing educational principles from sources as diverse as Plato, Sparta, Baden-Powell, and the British public school system, these two men made Salem one of the most famous schools in Europe. Hahn's mission was to foster extraordinarily well-rounded young men and women, distinguished from other students of their age by, among other things, "the gleam in their eyes." Words like "honour" and "equality" were taken very seriously. Children of the poor as well as the rich, slow learners with disabilities as well as the academically gifted, the physically inept as well as the naturally athletic — all were welcomed and all were encouraged, each to his or her greatest potential.

On two different occasions, the buildup of war brought Hahn closer to one of his destinies: the founding of the Outward Bound movement. In 1933 he was imprisoned by the Gestapo, only to be released through influential British connections and ensconced on Scotland's Moray Firth. By then he was almost 50, with no home, no job, and little money. What he lacked in these tangibles, however, he more than made up for in dreams and ideas. This time the result was a second school, housed in the castle at Gordonstoun, where among his first class of 13 young men was Prince Philip, later the Duke of Edinburgh. The school's proximity to the sea meant that water-based activities could become an extension of the school's playing fields. It also meant that students could become active participants in the Coast Guard network as well as the local Fire Brigade and Mountain Rescue Service.

At this time, too, a badge scheme was introduced — for athletic accomplishment, completing a sea or land expedition, working on some worthwhile long-term project, and/or service to the community. At first only Gordonstoun students were eligible, but soon the scheme was introduced to surrounding communities and was called the Moray Badge. From there it spread to the entire county and then to interested shires throughout England, where it became known as the County Badge scheme. Hahn's revolutionary ideas were gaining national credibility, and a number of influential commentators took up his cause.

In 1939, with war ever closer, the Moray Firth was thought to be in the path of a German invasion. Once again, Hahn and his school were forced to move. This time they went to the Welsh coast, where time, place, and circumstance were ripe for another beginning.

Within two years Hahn's new school was struggling. His Badge scheme had not caught on country-wide, and he dreamed of a new location where he could run a "short course," a residential programme of roughly a month's duration. Here young men could combine an outdoor experience with working towards the Badge.

And now other men entered the picture. Jim Hogan, an educator with ideals similar to Hahn's, an enabler who turned visions into realities, was first named secretary of the County Badge Experimental Committee and later first warden of the first Outward Bound school. Laurence Holt, a Gordonstoun parent and generous supporter and a director of Alfred Holt & Co., which ran the elite Blue Funnel Line, was keenly interested in training for the sea and sea survival. He coined the term "Outward Bound," which describes ships' crews leaving the certainties of home and embarking on bold adventures.

1941 • Hahn the dreamer, Holt the provider, and Hogan the facilitator establish the Aberdovey Sea School/Outward Bound Centre, which offers a 28-day residential course to demonstrate the efficacy of Hahn's County Badge ideas and provides for Holt's shipping companies a rapid training in survival after shipwreck. Bryneithyn, a grey stone house situated on a steep south-facing slope overlooking the Dovey Estuary, is purchased and adapted to its new role. Twenty-four boys enroll in the first course of the first Outward Bound centre.

1943 • Jim Hogan resigns and is followed by Freddie Fuller, an experienced seaman and small-boat sailor, and an excellent teacher and inspirer of the young. He writes: "At this very period when the world was filled with fear and hatred, this time when for this country it was the very winter of a deadly war, this new enterprise and School was born, lifting like the wild spring flower from the cold earth, with new promise and new hope." And later: "The great strength of these

Aberdovey Wharf

Casting off at Moray

7

early courses was team spirit and the growth of a sense of community. This was the contribution of Outward Bound to the survival of young people at sea during the war. Before the war's end, there was conviction that this had to be carried through to the days of peace. There was the realisation that the response of the boys attending courses at Aberdovey was much deeper than they had ever dreamed could develop."

1945 • World War II ends. Captain Fuller remembers sitting on the javelin field and having a discussion with Laurence Holt and one or two others about what should be done now that the war is over: "(We) agreed that Outward Bound was based on sound principles and that with certain modifications it could be made to work as well for other young men as it had for our sailors. We thought that we could find young people in considerable numbers in service clubs, schools, the uniformed services, and in industry." In fact, the industrial apprentices system, a tradition going back to the 13th century, continued to be the method by which many lads received their on-the-job training. Since they would remain with their firms for several years in a situation of mutual loyalty, any experience that would make them healthier, more alert, and therefore more productive would be as welcome to the sponsoring employers as to the participants. The logic proved irresistible, and apprentices became the backbone of the British Outward Bound schools; other recruits came from the armed forces, the police, and the fire service. Within a few years the training of these young men invariably included a month at Outward Bound.

1946 • The Outward Bound Trust is established, with an eye to expansion, to oversee fund-raising, publicity, and recruitment of staff and students. Its long-

Kayak construction
(girls' course at Bisham Abbey in 1959)

Campcraft at Bisham Abbey (1957)

time chairman is Sir Spencer Summers, a Conservative MP, whose energy, enthusiasm, and influence does a great deal to establish the Trust as an important and expanding force in British education.

The 1950s was the decade of Outward Bound expansion. Two mountain schools were established in England's Lake District, as were two other U.K. centres hundreds of miles apart in Scotland and Devon. Josh Miner, the father of Outward Bound U.S.A., came to know Kurt Hahn and his work firsthand. And Outward Bound schools were established on four continents, the products of Hahn's and the American-British Foundation of European Education's influence and the British Commonwealth network.

1950 • Eskdale, the U.K.'s first mountain school, opens in the Lake District; its first two wardens are mountaineers with international reputations.

• Josh Miner makes his initial trip to Gordonstoun and other institutions overseen by Kurt Hahn. He is particularly impressed with the Gordonstoun School Final Report to Parents: "The student was rated on his public spirit, sense of justice, and ability to follow out what he believed to be the right course in the face of various physical and psychological obstacles; on ability to state facts precisely, and to plan; on ability to organise — both as shown in the doing of his work and his direction of younger boys; on ability to deal with the unexpected; and on his conscientiousness — both in everyday affairs and in tasks with which he was especially entrusted. His imagination and manners were evaluated, as were his manual dexterity, the quality of his handicraft and other practical work, and the quality of his work in music, drawing, and other artistic endeavors. Then came the report on his academic performance and, if he were a member of the Cliff Watchers, the Fire Service, or the Army or Sea Cadets, a service report by his command officer."

1951 • The first all-girls' courses are held at Eskdale.

1951-52 • Miner teaches at Gordonstoun and becomes director of activities, which includes The Break: "Four mornings a week, during a 50-minute break . . . each boy took part in two of a half-dozen events — sprinting or distance running, long or high jumping, discus or javelin throwing. . . . He competed only against himself, trying to better his previous best performance."

1952 • The Moray Sea School receives its official Outward Bound charter.

• The Outward Bound Mountain School (East Africa) opens at Loitokitok on Mount Kilimanjaro.

• Germany's first sea school at Weissenhaus is established; it subsequently closes in the 1970s.

1953 • Kurt Hahn retires from Gordonstoun and pursues other educational interests, namely the Atlantic College.

• HRH the Duke of Edinburgh becomes Patron to Outward Bound.

1955 • Ullswater, a second U.K. mountain school set in the Lake District National Park, offers its first courses.

• The Outward Bound School Lumut is established on Malaysia's west coast.

1956 • Germany's first mountain school at Baad, technically in Austria, is founded.

1958 • Outward Bound Australia begins running courses at Fisherman's Point, north of Sydney.

1959 • The Devon school opens in southwestern England on the banks of the River Dart; it closes in the 1970s.

Freddie Fuller at Log Cabin during construction in the Dovey Forest.

9

Circuit training

The 1960s was the golden decade of Outward Bound. Two quite revolutionary programmes were set up in the U.K. Josh Miner's vow to bring Outward Bound to the United States was accomplished fivefold in just five years with many exciting applications, and seven more schools on four continents were added to the Outward Bound world directory.

1960 • The Netherlands opens a sea school, and it rapidly changes with the times.

• Hahn's first Atlantic College is established in Wales.

1961 • Zimbabwe's first Outward Bound school is called the Outward Bound Association of Central Africa and covers what is now Zimbabwe, Zambia, and Malawi.

1962 • New Zealand's Cobham Outward Bound School is instituted on the northeast corner of the nation's South Island.

• Colorado Outward Bound School, set in the Rocky Mountains and the first in the Western Hemisphere, is founded and begins a U.S. tradition of involvement with inner-city youth that continues to this day.

1963 • The Outward Bound Trust of the U.K. authorises the use of the Outward Bound title in the U.S., which allows Colorado and subsequent U.S. schools official Outward Bound status.

• Rhowniar, just north of Aberdovey, is purchased for the exclusive use of girls.

1964 • Zambia's Outward Bound Lake School in Mbala is converted from a coffee plantation and hotel near the southern end of Lake Tanganyika.

• Minnesota's Outward Bound School, later called Voyageur, begins running courses on the Canadian border.

• U.S. schools begin work with adjudicated youth.

1964-65 • Hurricane Island, a sea school off the coast of Maine, begins operation.

1965 • The U.S. Outward Bound Board of Trustees sees its mission as twofold: to enter the mainstream of American education and life and to adopt the policy of Outreach, in Josh Miner's words, "to venture beyond itself to proselyte institutions capable of multiplying its influence."

• The first all-women's courses in the U.S. begin at Voyageur.

• Trenton, New Jersey's Action Bound program sends 30 urban youths to Colorado, Minnesota, and Hurricane Island, the first step in an effective relationship between the two organisations.

1966 • The Massachusetts Division of Youth Services works closely with U.S. Outward Bound schools, with "statistically significant" results.

• Northwest Outward Bound school, later Pacific Crest, begins running courses in the Pacific Northwest of the U.S.

1967 • City Challenge, a true Outward Bound revolution, is devised by Freddie Fuller after his work with American Peace Corps training. In Jim Hogan's words: "The slums of Puerto Rico presented a challenge to the Peace Corps volunteers at least equal to that they met in the rivers and jungles. Freddie came home convinced that it would be possible to devise a course for young people in an urban setting in which they would be faced with tasks just as demanding as those they had tackled on the sea and in the mountains. I must confess the scepticism with which I first reacted to this idea; in the end, however, Freddie overwhelmed me with his faith."

• The Outward Bound School Singapore is inaugurated on the island of Pulau Ubin, 15 kilometres from the city centre.

• North Carolina Outward Bound establishes its base camp under Table Rock Mountain in the western part of the state.

• Colorado Outward Bound and Denver East High School begin a far-reaching educational mainstream partnership.

1968 • Germany's second mountain school, at Berchtesgaden, is opened.

1969 • Outward Bound Western Canada, then known as OB British Columbia, starts operations in Keremeos, B.C.

• The first coeducational courses in the U.S. begin at Voyageur.

• The first coeducational courses in the U.K. begin at Rhowniar.

• Dartmouth Center is established at Dartmouth University in New Hampshire; it subsequently closes.

• Outward Bound meets Upward Bound at Wesleyan University in Connecticut, "the successful start of a significant strand in the Outreach story of Outward Bound U.S.A. . . . one of the longest-running and most successful Outward Bound collaborations," in which economically and culturally deprived ninth graders, identified as possessing college potential, experience firsthand a Standard Outward Bound course at North Carolina.

Tom Price, a 30-year veteran of Outward Bound as instructor and warden on four continents, perhaps sums up the 1960s for Outward Bound staff at that time: "To those of us who worked in the schools in those days, life felt rich. Work to us was like play to small children; the more serious and earnest it is, the greater the fun and excitement. Each course was like a little life-time of experience, and when it ended we were left deflated and drained, often with only a day or so before we had to wind up to the next."

The 1970s was a period of cutback and retrenchment. Schools/centres were closed, moved, and/or consolidated in both the U.K. and the U.S. Internationally, however, schools continued to open in North America, Asia, Africa, and on the European continent.

1970 • The Hong Kong Outward Bound School begins operations at its Tai Mong Tsai headquarters, situated on the northeastern tip of the New Territories.

• The first winter courses are held in the U.S., at Voyageur Outward Bound School, heralding the advent of year-round operations.

• Texas Outward Bound School, later Southwest Outward Bound, is established; it subsequently closes.

1972 • Outward Bound Netherlands is reorganised and transfers its operations to Ulvenhout.

1973 • Outward Bound Australia moves to the bush of the Australian Capital Territory; five years later its permanent base is established nearby.

1975 • An Outward Bound centre is inaugurated in Lesotho, a country completely surrounded by the Republic of South Africa.

1976 • Loch Eil opens in the Scottish Highlands after the closure and "move" of the Moray Sea School.

• The Canadian Outward Bound Wilderness School, the lone outpost on Black Sturgeon Lake in northern Ontario, runs its first courses.

• Aberdovey and Rhowniar centres join forces, and Outward Bound Wales is formed.

1977 • The Belgian Outward Bound School is founded.

1979 • The Outward Bound School Lumut in Malaysia moves its base to a more remote area.

• Tanzanian Outward Bound Centre is opened on the southeastern slopes of Mount Kilimanjaro, due to the closure of the border between Kenya and Tanzania.

In the 1970s U.S. Outreach commitment begins to focus (and, in the 1990s, continues to focus) on three other major constituents: the urban

Fire drill at Aberdovey

disadvantaged through Urban Outward Bound bases (now) in Minneapolis/St. Paul, Chicago, Boston, Baltimore, Los Angeles, San Francisco, San Diego, and Atlanta; industry with its design and implementation of management training and professional development courses; and special-needs groups whereby specialist courses, based on need and demand, are (now) held for, among others, the physically disabled and blind, substance abusers, victims of domestic violence, Vietnam veterans suffering from Post Trauma Stress Disorder, academic underachievers, gifted high school students, and recovering cancer patients.

Perhaps the most radical directions Outward Bound took in the 1980s were realised in the two greatly diverse locations of New York City and New Zealand. The former established the first wholly urban center, anticipating a new city-wilderness commitment by Outward Bound; the latter hosted the first international conference, a precursor and acknowledgment of the importance of a cohesive international movement.

1983 • New Zealand hosts the first international Outward Bound conference celebrating the rebuilding of the centre at Anakiwa and 21 years in operation.
• The Netherlands institutes its City Bound project.
1985 • The Outward Bound School Kinarut, Malaysia, opens on the island of Borneo after a three-year clearing and building project.
1986 • The Outward Bound School Lumut, Malaysia, is the site of the second international conference.
1987 • Outward Bound Zimbabwe is re-established after a ten-year hiatus due to the unstable political situation in the area.
• Hors Limites Outward Bound France is founded, the first organisation to follow

procedures for affiliate members formulated at the Malaysian conference.
• The New York City Outward Bound Center is established, the only independently chartered urban center in the world.
• The International Secretariat is formed, following the mandate of the second international conference.
1988 • Outward Bound Western Canada reorganises and moves ten hours distant, to Pemberton, British Columbia.
• Outward Bound Konigsburg, Germany's new sea school, enrolls its first students on a site adjacent to the Baltic Sea.
• The third international conference is held at Cooperstown, New York, resulting in the formation of an International Advisory Board with regional representation and in an internationally-agreed mission statement.
1989 • Outward Bound Japan becomes a reality after twenty years as a vision.
• Harvard Graduate School of Education initiates a joint venture with Outward Bound U.S.A. over a three-year period to implant the Outward Bound experience-based teaching approach into public education in a variety of meaningful ways: a course based on the pedagogy of Kurt Hahn will be offered, a chair will be endowed in the field of experiential learning, and educators from throughout the country will be able to attend practica on an ongoing basis.

The Outward Bound 1990s begin like the 1940s, at Aberdovey in Wales, this time to celebrate 50 years of Outward Bound.
1991 • The fourth international conference is held at Aberdovey: delegates from many of the organisation's 32 schools/centres in 18 countries on 5 continents attend the celebration.

Ian Fothergill, Director of the Outward Bound Trust in the United Kingdom, makes some personal remarks about the future:

The growth of Outward Bound throughout the world has been phenomenal. Equally phenomenal is its amazing commonality of language. Despite course differences necessitated by social, geographical, and climatic variables, the organisation's tradition remains concerned with communal support, a bombardment of challenge, making people know that there is more in them than they previously believed, that group effort can be harnessed for the ultimate good of the individual, that everyone can learn and grow. The influence of Outward Bound, too, has been very significant and has extended far beyond the movement itself. Thus, a far greater mission than perhaps even Kurt Hahn could have envisioned has been fulfilled.

To look to the future, we must look upward and outward. But we must also look to the past, back to basics which at the time, it must be remembered, were quite revolutionary. Any Outward Bound experience encompasses four components: clients and courses, which must be considered together; staff; and facilities.

First and second, we must look more and more to client needs while maintaining a clear vision of Outward Bound values. We began by serving a youthful population in 1941, but the youth of today present far different challenges. So we must design more specific, tailor-made packages to reach them from different angles with new strategies. Our present mission to youth worldwide is to get through to as wide a cross-section as possible. Disadvantaged

HRH Prince Philip and Prince Louis

youth represent a substantial percentage of the world's population, and we simply cannot afford to cut ourselves off from such a significant proportion of our future.

But we have other clients as well. Our corporate customers in industry and commerce have always been major sponsors and beneficiaries of our work. Recent trends have seen the development of specific courses — team-building, leadership, and the like — for an older, more mature group. Again, we must tailor experience to fit particular needs. Two trends must be encouraged: specialised staff development and dedicated facilities. Special-needs courses are also being developed successfully for special clients at many centres around the world involving people disadvantaged physically and/or mentally, and there are specifically designed programmes for older groups.

Third, in each country we must encourage a key team of staff open to new ideas and developments. We must recruit a much wider range of personnel representing specific constituencies — ethnic minorities, the inner city, the corporate world, the handicapped — who can intimately understand and better work with our diverse clientele. They should all become experts in the Outward Bound process, be conversant with technical skills as well as being committed to supporting people in a residential community.

Last, the issue of facilities is immensely variable and dependent on local issues and environments. World-wide, they range from millions of pounds worth of country estates and grounds to two tents and a national park, shared with all. Diversity here will undoubtedly remain.

HRH Prince Philip and Devon students

Bowsprit of Prince Louis

14

Facilities are somewhat bound up with the issue of environment, one topic of four others including safety, education, and expansion which I also wish to address.

There has been no "greening" of Outward Bound, simply because we have always been "green." The wilderness — of sea and land — has always been our environment; we have had to preserve it to survive. Environmental concerns have been at the heart of much of our community service emphasis around the globe. Now, it must be admitted that not everyone of our clients will experience the wilderness. New environments must thus be discovered — and some have been. Most significantly, the new wilderness is the inner city, where environmental issues, though very different, are equally important.

Physical safety has always been our greatest concern. Today, the term safety also takes into account individuals' emotional and mental well-being. Our participants must be assured of a caring, supportive environment whenever and wherever they come into contact with Outward Bound. Detailed safety manuals, research committees, and the advice of experts will always be of primary importance to our mission.

More and more of the methods and philosophy of Outward Bound have found their way into the world's educational systems, complementing more formal, traditional teaching methods. In several countries Outward Bound organisations have identified their primary mission as securing a place in mainstream education itself as part of the school curriculum. Experiential teaching and participatory learning have been absorbed into developmentally-based education schemes around the globe.

International expansion sounds good, but is never easy, and will require a controversial mix of flexibility and perhaps some loss of autonomy. Globally, the next few years should see new centres primarily in the Middle and Far East and in Eastern Europe. In fact, Outward Bound preparation committees are at work now in several of these areas, and we are looking at ways to foster local initiatives through them. But we must face this issue of autonomy head-on; that is the real challenge for the future. At the very least we should build on common strengths and seek out common goals. Of course, this is far more easily accomplished in some areas or regions than in others. One model might be the European Executive by which the five Outward Bound countries of Europe are linked. It encourages consistency, quality of product, and marketing skills as each nation looks forward to 1992 and the European Community.

Finally, I wish to endorse with the greatest enthusiasm the "Mission Statement" presented to the Third International Conference held at Cooperstown, New York, in 1988. We must: seek to inspire self-respect, care for others, responsibility to the community and sensitivity to the world environment; proclaim our belief in the value of compassion through active help for human beings; promote greater understanding between people, especially the young, of different races and cultures; work together on an international basis to remove the barriers which separate the people of the world.

Ian Fothergill
DIRECTOR, OUTWARD BOUND TRUST

The Wharf and the Dovey Estuary

Gliding past 10th-century Castle Coeffin, a cutter from Outward Bound Loch Eil crosses the Sound of Mull.

United Kingdom

ABERDOVEY is synonymous with Outward Bound. Its co-founders, Kurt Hahn and Laurence Holt, and its first two wardens, Jim Hogan and Freddie Fuller, shaped the place and the movement 50 years ago on a 50-acre site looking out over the Dovey Estuary in mid-Wales.

Aberdovey was established as a Sea School "to provide a rigorous, adventurous, pre-sea training course for young men who might go on to help with the Battle of the Atlantic." After meeting its initial goals, the school continued to do a great deal more. From the beginning, community service has been an important part of the programme, especially in the arenas of sea and mountain rescue. For example, the local lifeboat is crewed by both villagers and Outward Bound staff, and students may be called upon to participate in mountain rescue activities.

Today, a full-time professional staff of more than 30 tutors works with up to 120 students at a time on a year-round basis. Activities fill the spectrum on land and water: rock climbing and abseiling, hillwalking and expeditions, orienteering, canoeing and sailing and kayaking and raft-building. Ropes courses, including the zip wire, are complemented by the "soft" skills of review, discussion, reflection, and the solo.

Would Hahn and Holt recognise what they had wrought 50 years ago? Indisputably. Bryneithyn, the old stone house, has weathered many a gale, as has Outward Bound itself. Much has changed; the essence remains the same.

"Self-awakening. This is the strength of an Outward Bound course. This sets people on fire years afterward. People in their 50s, successful in their lives, careers, families — they talk of their experience of Outward Bound as if it were only yesterday. As one person expressed, 'There seems to be a light within me, which may dim from time to time, but keeps flaming up. . . .' I remember happily from a distance of almost 50 years how quickly I and the young men of 1943, intent upon a sea career, accepted each other with warm exchanges and a common goal — to give and to serve. They gave me much joy as I observed their development — so helpful, willing and selfless, with concern and care for others."

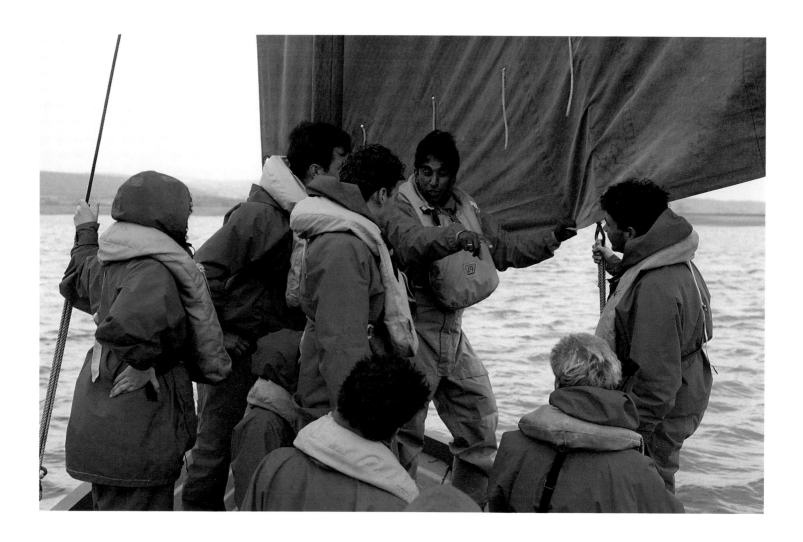

*Learning basic seamanship, students prepare to set sail on
the Dovey Estuary. The waters around Aberdovey offer
challenge and variety, primary considerations in choosing
this site for the first Outward Bound centre.*

This new generation of fibreglass cutter is moulded from the original hull of traditional coastal vessels used here 50 years ago.

Bracing himself for a seal launch, a student must trust his teammates to lift a platform carefully, plunging his kayak into high tide.

A group from Aberdovey learns kayaking technique, and a Rhowniar student passes precariously from jetty to shore in a modified bosun's chair.

The soft glow of early morning illuminates the western slopes of Cader Idris as a management group responds to a staged emergency alert. Delegates have been given only 14 hours to learn the necessary skills to carry out this complex rescue operation.

*Once the "casualty" has been located, students rush to provide aid
and comfort. The team, guided by radio, carefully lowers ropes as the
barrow boy eases the stretcher down the steep mountainside.*

To provide a centre exclusively for young women, the Trust purchased in 1963 a substantial and elegant property called RHOWNIAR. It consisted of a "family house of some character" and 55 acres, with formal gardens. Individual courses for women had been organised at several U.K. centres from the early 1950s. The demand grew, and a separate facility was deemed the most appropriate solution.

From the start there was felt to be something indefinably unique about the school. Although located just three and a half miles from Aberdovey and half a mile from the open sea, the "feeling" was somehow quite different. It has been described as "the school with a soul," its setting and atmosphere contemplative and thought-provoking, its environment having a major influence on all who come into contact with it.

It was at Rhowniar in January 1969 that the first Outward Bound coeducational courses were held. One eyewitness recounted: "All were wearing anoraks and trousers and some of the boys had long hair, so it was often difficult to tell the boys from the girls. . . . There had been some fears that a Standard course would be too strenuous for the girls, but I saw no sign of this. . . . (In fact), near the end of the course I thought (their) 'staying power' was on the whole rather better than that of the boys." From the beginning the experiences offered have been considered to be particularly well-rounded. Formal drama productions have evolved into workshops using drama-based group exercises to enhance the personal development elements of the courses. Other activities include rock climbing, overnight expedition, and the solo, often sited in and around four mountain log cabins located 10 to 15 miles from the centre.

*Hurling himself from a treetop platform, a Rhowniar student flies
along Europe's longest zip wire into the expanse of forest beyond.*

Like a tightrope walker suspended high above the valley floor, a young girl carefully balances each step to steady the "Burma Bridge."

"Your disability is your opportunity" — *Kurt Hahn's words ring true for a developmentally disabled student as she overcomes her fear while climbing a rock face.*

OUTWARD BOUND ESKDALE is situated in the picturesque valley of the River Esk, in the remote high fells of England's western Lake District. Its proximity to some of the best rock climbing in the country near Scafell Pike, the highest in England, is an added bonus. The centre itself provides everything of necessity for participants. It is set in a splendid 24-hectare garden complete with a small tarn and includes Lord Rea's Victorian/Edwardian turreted mansion, called Gatehouse, and several outbuildings.

Eskdale has always been justifiably proud of its mountain men and women, wardens and staff with international reputations, who have seldom been satisfied to remain Lakeland-bound all their Outward Bound careers. This fact remains true to the present day, as the widely experienced Eskdale staff, who for the most part are in their late 20s to late 30s, contribute to a reputation for a particular expertise in working with adults. Additionally, they are at the forefront of strengthening links with a number of outdoor education organisations in Eastern Europe.

Another facet of the centre's special strength lies in its innovative course development. Eskdale currently has developed more than 60 tailor-made courses for any number of clientele: from managers ripe for development to substance abusers; from rock climbing enthusiasts to the "Old But Bold" over-50s; from diabetics, asthmatics and those afflicted with serious visual impairment to the Outward Bound Manchester Project, sponsored by Esso and TSB, which might include a group of women on probation.

Nestled in the valley beneath England's highest peak, Eskdale's main centre offers a picturesque view of canoeists on the tarn.

"It's never too late to change direction" — *a recurring theme in the Old But Bold programme. Here, a student strives to sustain balance and strength on crossover ropes.*

Reassured by her tutor, an elderly woman leans backward over a precipice to descend the vertical face.

With coaxing from fellow students, a young woman plunges from Dalegarth Leap, braced for her icy descent to the narrow river below.

*Without verbal communication, a team of managers needs ingenuity
and original thinking to advance "The Caterpillar."*

Perhaps the only thing whimsical about OUTWARD BOUND ULLSWATER is its discovery. In 1955, grants from various trusts made possible the establishment of a second mountain school. The search committee, after a hard day looking for an appropriate site in England's Lake District, stopped for tea at an old lakeside hotel. In conversation with the landlord, the committee's needs and desires were made known, the hotel itself was found to be for sale, and a bargain was struck on the spot.

What they got was a dignified 18th-century house on the north shore of Lake Ullswater near Watermillock, nine miles from Penrith in the heart of the Lake District National Park. On the "other side" of Lakeland and over one and a half hours distant from Eskdale, this mountain centre could boast a large lake at its feet with a boathouse and jetty and superb access to a large area of unspoilt upland countryside.

In more recent years, Ullswater has concentrated a great deal of its energies on courses with a management and adult emphasis. In fact, about 70 percent of its courses deal in some way with corporate development, and 80 percent of its clientele is sponsored by organisations. A large number of both national and international companies have made long-term commitments to Outward Bound courses at Ullswater as an integral part of their employee training packages. Special features include pre-course, company-based briefings for corporate development courses, and the pioneering, with Eskdale, of "Old But Bold," courses for persons over 50.

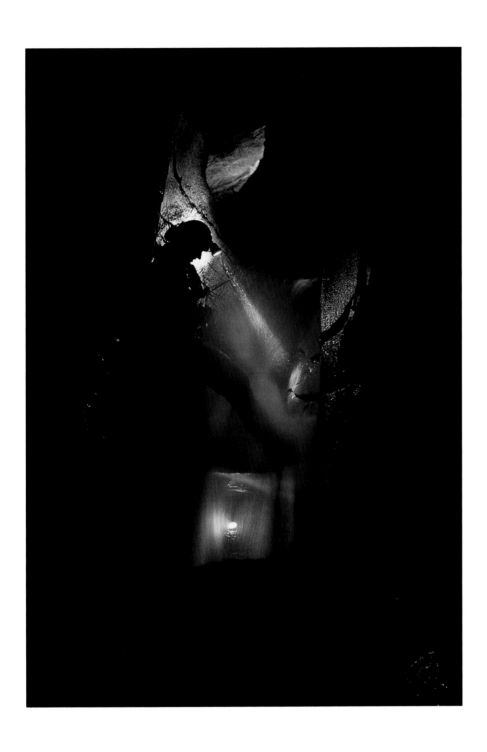

Known as the Three Peaks, this area of the Yorkshire Dales National Park is pocked with countless limestone caves. Through dark caverns of cold rock, students must find the route that forces them up a water chute by rope and escape through an open shaft far above.

Kayak jumping builds confidence in the power of teamwork for a management group training on the lake at Ullswater.

Young students race four and a half miles over rugged,
mountainous terrain at Gowbarrow Fell.

Engineering apprentices tackle "The Wall" in their effort to scale the
15-foot smooth surface without the aid of ropes or equipment.

"From my earliest involvement with Outward Bound I was excited by its effectiveness in bringing to people a greater understanding of themselves and their relationships with others. The dual components of service and striving in Outward Bound's motto 'to serve, to strive and not to yield' summarised well my hopes for a world in which a climate of compassion and community could act as context for individuals who felt satisfied and worthy from having discovered, and then achieved, according to their true potentials."

The centre base of OUTWARD BOUND LOCH EIL is a grand 18th-century shooting lodge on the north shore of the loch. The site accommodates 90 in student dormitories, while another 90 students may be out on mobile expeditionary courses.

Two of these courses, unique to Loch Eil, are aptly called Viking Wayfarer and Skye Trek. The former is planned for 12 days in 28-foot open boats and explores loch, sound, and small islands up and down the coast; the latter is a 12-day backpacking trip through remote areas of the Isle of Skye, crossing the Cuillin Ridge.

Notable special course successes of recent years have involved the Glasgow Inner City Project, which includes pre-course preparation, a preliminary centre visit, and post-course follow-up; groups of young people coming together from different communities in Belfast; and those suffering from cerebral palsy and Down's syndrome, "youngsters most looked forward to by all staff members."

Groups of 12 at base and no more than 10 on mobile courses, both called clans, partake of a feast of activities. These might include hillwalking, mountain expeditions, rock climbing, winter mountaincraft, both flat- and white-water canoeing, coastal expeditionary sailing or day sailing, and service projects such as repairing farmers' fences and volunteer work at the local hospital.

Just recently a new 50-year lease on the property has been signed with the Dulverton Trust, enabling Loch Eil to proceed with its future concerns. These include its willingness to share facilities with European Outward Bound centres and to share expertise with Eastern Europeans who are eager to transplant Outward Bound to their countries.

Outward Bound programmes are not easy and are not meant to be. They are designed so that everyone can succeed at their own level, if they have the willingness to try.

Loch Eil's 12-day trek on the Isle of Skye, one of the most remote wilderness areas in Western Europe, culminates with the spectacular Alpine terrain of the Cuillin Ridge in the Scottish Hebrides.

*Students row ashore to camp beneath the ruins of Castle Achandun
during an eight-day cutter expedition from Loch Eil to Loch Linnhe.*

Learning by doing, crews develop endurance and independence. When students prove capable of manoeuvring the vessel in conditions that can vary dramatically, the expedition is completed without instruction.

Clinging mist shrouds the hilltops, casting eerie shadows on the Lynn
of Morvern. The real adventure, however, takes place in the hearts
and minds of those who embark on an inward journey.

What Freddie Fuller pioneered in 1967 was truly revolutionary for the Outward Bound movement. For three weeks in July of that year he replaced the challenges of the sea with those of urban decay and despair. He, Jim Hogan, Outward Bound staff, and local youth leaders encouraged a group of 37 young men to confront the inner city of Leeds and themselves on a programme that would change forever many things and people, including Outward Bound. Its name: CITY CHALLENGE.

The idea was born of Fuller's training programmes for the American Peace Corps in Puerto Rico. Upon his return to England, he was keen to translate his success into an Outward Bound experience. As Fuller noted, British "cities were a wilderness in which challenges could be found for young people. . . . The sentiment of compassion was not a popular one, but we made sure it had a place in Outward Bound."

Today, who avails themselves of these experiences and what exactly do they do? A typical 12-day course divides 40 men and women aged 17 to 24 into groups of eight. They live together at a residential school in an inner city area and take part in two or three contrasting placements. These might include a hostel for the homeless, a psychiatric ward in a city hospital, and in-home assistance for physically challenged people. A hands-on project is also encouraged. Each evening powerful follow-up group review sessions and discussions are held to explore in-depth the activities themselves and themes of prejudice, disability awareness, and racism.

"I now have the confidence to get to grips with all the things that I once thought were beyond me. The course has completely changed my attitude, not only to work, but to people and life itself."

Ranging from lush rainforest to the barren expanse of the Yaggerup Dunes, the spectrum of Australian terrain provides a unique backdrop for the Outward Bound experience.

Australia / New Zealand

OUTWARD BOUND AUSTRALIA is unique for any number of reasons. Courses operate in all states of mainland Australia, from tropical North Queensland to the Snowy Mountains, from the southern shores of Victoria to arid Central Australia, from the canyons of New South Wales to the wilderness of southwest Western Australia. No wonder it is a tradition of Australian Outward Bound that all courses involve a wide range of activities with no single activity predominant.

At the present time, fully 80 percent of all school offerings may be termed contract courses. Amongst the most sophisticated of these are the individually designed Management Training and Corporate Development Programmes. Another major area of operation is in the field of education, where Outward Bound Australia has built a strong reputation for both high school experiential learning programs and teacher training and development at the university level.

Outward Bound Australia places a strong emphasis on Australia-wide operational and communications systems and national standard operating procedures and safety policies. They have found this absolutely essential given the vast distances, the diversity of activities, and the large numbers and wide range of clients.

Other common threads that hold Outward Bound Australia together are its distinctive staff policies, which work strongly on a multiple skill and responsibility principle, and its emphasis on the role of social science research, including an extensive in-house computerized reference library.

A student embarks on his solo experience. Here he will spend three days of a 26-day course in isolation on the Great Barrier Reef.

PHOTOGRAPH: GUY PRITCHARD

Where wind and waves sculpt the ancient shoreline of Western Australia, an expedition winds through Nornalup National Park. Nornalup is an aboriginal term meaning "place of the black snakes."

During an expedition in New South Wales, a young wallaby is spotted peering from its mother's pouch. In remote wilderness areas, students often encounter fauna unique to this fascinating continent.

Rock climbing, one of the few activities that students face alone, is an experience that tests them physically, emotionally, and spiritually.

Karri trees in Western Australia provide an ideal place for abseil training. The largest of a thousand Eucalyptus varieties, this giant looms 30 metres above the forest floor.

57

In stark contrast to rock and sky, a student takes in the panorama from her vantage point, free-abseiling from cliffs high above the Indian Ocean.

Trekking the Snowy Mountains in Victoria, students use their newly-acquired orienteering skills to navigate 300 kilometres of trackless bush.

Fostering determination and perseverance, Outward Bound programmes offer young people a chance to leave behind the safe harbours of family and routine to face the uncomfortable, the difficult, and the adventurous.

To add variety and challenge to mobile wilderness courses, Outward Bound Australia has developed original methods of moving groups and gear. Raftsailing demands both skill and stamina to manoeuvre in the high winds of Nornalup Inlet.

Canoeists negotiate rapids on the Murrumbidgee River en route to the Tharwa base camp, the Outward Bound National centre in the Australian Capital Territory.

With personal gear tucked beneath them, students ride the rapids on air mattresses, cascading in northern New South Wales.

New Zealand's COBHAM OUTWARD BOUND SCHOOL has enjoyed powerful support and national appeal since its inception in 1961-62. A Council and Trust were established at an inaugural meeting at Government House. Backed by influential business interests, financing was found nationwide and active local committees were set up at once.

The group's first responsibility was soon discharged: the purchase of a centre base, a hotel and 18 hectares at Anakiwa near Picton, in a sheltered recess of Queen Charlotte Sound at the northeast corner of the country's South Island. The site and its surrounds have been described as "a mixture of Norway, Austria, the Riviera, and the South Sea Islands."

One result of this unique grass-roots involvement has been the direction the centre has taken in promoting a healthy cross-section of clients and courses. The Council actively encourages the participation of Maoris, New Zealand's indigenous population, and others of Pacific Islands descent, so that currently 20 percent of participants are from these groups. Then, too, a number of courses are designed and run for the intellectually and physically challenged. An annual Teachers' Practicum is also held, and educators across the country are invited to discover the value of experiential learning in teaching.

New Zealand's Cobham Outward Bound School hosted the first International Conference in 1983 and an international Standard course in 1991, celebrating 50 years of Outward Bound.

Overlooking the school centre and neighbouring town of Anakiwa, an indigenous New Zealander climbs an outcrop of the Iwitauroa Ridge. Iwitauroa is a Maori term meaning "challenge."

Casting fear aside, a student leans backwards to fall from a height into the arms of his watchmates. This group bonding exercise is known as the "trust fall."

Sheep roam freely on the 26-acre school farm in New Zealand's South Island as students confront "The Wall."

The school's 32-foot cutters have alternating work stations for 14 students. Without winches or mechanical advantages, "if it doesn't blow, you row."

Following the route of Captain Cook into an area rich in Maori history, The Resolution *is a vessel similar to the one he used to explore the Marlborough Sounds in the late 1700s.*

Intense concentration shows on the face of a native Maori student traversing a precarious rope bridge over a pool of mud.

Mornings at Anakiwa begin early. An exercise session and a two-mile run end in the dawn mist of Okiwa Bay, making an exhilarating start to the day of discovery that lies ahead.

The Outward Bound School Kinarut boasts a half-mile strand of golden beach on the South China Sea.

Asia

The OUTWARD BOUND SCHOOL KINARUT, in Sabah, East Malaysia, on the island of Borneo, is an intriguing mix of the traditional and the forward-thinking.

The school's numerous activities are enviably based in the mountains and jungles and on both fresh- and salt-water rivers and the nearby sea. All are used on the 26-day Standard course, one of the few remaining at any Outward Bound school in the world.

Kurt Hahn's original four "pillars" are incorporated into almost every programme at Kinarut: emphases on physical fitness, self-reliance, public service, and project work. Much of the last consists of construction projects in and around the school, largely designed by the students themselves, with little staff supervision.

Here is where the traditional begins to become quite innovative. Unlike most of the world's Outward Bound schools, students at Kinarut are not equipped for their expedition. At the end of a walking day in the jungle and in the tradition of the people of the interior of Borneo, the students use their parang knives to cut wood from the jungle. They build a frame, tie it together with string from creepers, and place a tarpaulin over it. They sleep communally in their "longhouse" tents and cook over traditional campfires.

One of the school's more unique public services is the encouragement of blood donations from students between the ages of 17 and 55. Then, too, this school in the most multi-racial state in the world, with 24 distinct ethnic groups, prides itself on its ethnically diverse staff and its increasing international representation. Course participants from throughout the world are numbered among Kinarut's alumni, in spite of its site being one of the most remote of the Outward Bound schools.

Through sailing, students find a greater awareness about themselves and their fellow crew members, and develop respect, affection, and trust.

The rain forests of Sabah become a wilderness classroom; the expedition is a journey of self-discovery and personal growth.

In the tradition of Borneo's indigenous people, students use parang knives to clear pathways through dense jungle and to build overnight shelters.

Working together towards a common goal, students from Sabah's many ethnic groups help each other over "The Wall."

"Being caught up in a movement that is characterised by high energy, boldness, and resilience. The meaning for me comes in flashbacks! A legless man on a zip wire, the anguish of an instructor who has lost a student. Blind people on the top of Kilimanjaro, a CEO of a major corporation saying, 'This is simply the best thing that ever happened to me.' "

Malaysia's OUTWARD BOUND SCHOOL LUMUT has a proud history. It is one of the first extant centres established outside the U.K. and the only school to run 10 Standard courses a year for the last 36 years.

It was in 1954 that a site was chosen by its first warden, G.W. Fuller, "80 man-sized paces from the sea" on Malaysia's west coast in the state of Perak. It was located there until 1979 when the site was needed as a naval base, and it has more recently moved to a nearby isolated bay surrounded by islands, sandy beaches, rivers, hills, forests, and small fishing communities.

From the very beginning, all financial assistance was provided by donations from the private sector and individuals; no government funding has been accepted. Today, Outward Bound Lumut remains self-funded, independent, and secular.

From the beginning, too, its purpose was clear. Founded in the interest of the future of the country and its multi-racial society composed of Malays, Chinese, Indians, Eurasians, and Europeans, its programme was tailored to national needs. Today, it remains "multi-national, like the nation, where students and staff have contributed since 1955 to promoting integration, unity, and good citizenship."

Today, too, the centre is especially proud of its facilities, its staff, and its curriculum. Its 13-acre site includes a variety of purpose-built structures capable of accommodating 140 participants. The centre is completely self-contained. The average tenure of a participant is an astounding 20 days, which attests to the demand for the 25-day Standard course for 16-year-olds and up.

Students at the Outward Bound School Lumut struggle to sustain the cadence required to hold true the vessel's course in calm waters.

*A splash of colour off the island of Pangkor, a kayaking expedition
puts to sea in Western Malaysia.*

Communication and teamwork are keys to unlocking the human knot.

A 10-year-old boy peers from his makeshift shelter in anticipation of the night ahead. Other students camp only 30 feet away, but without words between them, he is essentially alone.

Reinforcing his bivouac with coconut fronds, a young student prepares for his solo adventure.

The OUTWARD BOUND SCHOOL SINGAPORE is located at the northeastern tip of Singapore on the island of Pulau Ubin. Known as "Stone Mountain" because of its rich granite resources, it is an isolated spot, both rustic and rugged, yet just 15 kilometres from the city itself.

Most parts of the island, embracing the surrounding forests and an old quarry, are used for the school's numerous land-based activities. Other parts of Singapore and the surrounding islands are all used for the school's comprehensive water-based programme.

Outward Bound Singapore offers a comprehensive curriculum, one that is fully utilised by its clientele, a large percentage of whom are young students and civil servants and members of the uniformed services. In 1967, the need was seen to train the youth of Singapore (where half the population is under 21) and build a more physically rugged and mentally tenacious people. The programmes have an added value for a multi-racial society such as Singapore's. Training affords an excellent opportunity to build team spirit regardless of the participants' race, sex, and cultural and social background.

The management of Outward Bound Singapore was handed over to the People's Association on 1 April 1991. PA is now re-developing the school into a modern adventure training centre, while maintaining the Outward Bound concept. Still, its mission remains consistent: to develop Singapore's most precious natural resource, its youth.

Far removed from concrete and steel, Singapore students develop confidence in unknown situations and new respect for nature in the mud walk.

*Trusting rope and trainer, a student runs down the steep
rock face of an old quarry.*

Jetty jumping helps students confront their fears, which are mostly imagined and self-imposed.

To appreciate fully the dedication and vision of the first Outward Bound school established in Asia that does not trace its history back to Britain's colonial roots, both the past and future of OUTWARD BOUND JAPAN must be explored. The Outward Bound concept was first introduced in 1972 when Outward Bound Japan's current chairman, Koichi Inasawa, attended the Junior Chamber Asian Conference and heard of the Malaysian Outward Bound School.

An Outward Bound Japan board was organised with Inasawa acting as chairman. From 1975 onward, pilot Outward Bound courses were offered on an annual basis. In the spring of 1989, the first permanent Outward Bound Japan school was established in Nagano, with staff from Outward Bound Colorado, Hong Kong, and New Zealand assisting with the courses. Nearly 20 years after the vision, Outward Bound Japan had become a reality.

The Nagano School is located in the peaceful mountain village of Otari, nestled between two national parks 20 kilometres south of the Japan Sea. Mountains (to 3,000 metres and snow-covered from December through March), marshlands, and fresh-water lakes all guarantee a diverse choice of activities and a wide range of courses; hot springs and edible Alpine plants lend an exotic touch.

Outward Bound Japan seeks to serve society by instilling in its youth courage, self-confidence, a sense of personal responsibility, and increased appreciation of the natural environment, and by cultivating national leaders in outdoor education.

Shu Kawashina, brother of Princess Kiko, participates in group orientation at Outward Bound Japan's base camp on the first day of a youth leadership course.

PHOTOGRAPH: OUTWARD BOUND JAPAN

The Alpine panorama is a breathtaking backdrop for this group on its final expedition. Having tested themselves to new limits, students of all ages return to their familiar lives with greater insight and motivation.

PHOTOGRAPH: OUTWARD BOUND JAPAN

Rugged mountains surrounding the Nagano school offer superb climbing opportunities for Japanese students.

PHOTOGRAPH: OUTWARD BOUND JAPAN

OUTWARD BOUND HONG KONG is in a number of enviable positions.

The school's two land/sea bases are both set in secluded areas of outstanding natural beauty. The brand-new Sir Murray MacLehose Training Base is sited on a remote island at the southern end of Double Haven in Mirs Bay. Tai Mong Tsai headquarters is situated on the northeastern tip of the New Territories. Superb facilities include accommodation and catering blocks for trainees and staff and splendid land- and water-based equipment.

The 132-foot brigantine *Ji Fung*, "The Spirit of Resolution," is also moored here. Built less than a decade ago with funds provided by the Royal Hong Kong Jockey Club, it can accommodate from 36 to 40 in four cabins, in addition to a staff of eight. Its setting is the South China Sea.

Outward Bound Hong Kong is also fortunate in the present strength of its financial and alumni support. This means the school can continue its commitment to ensure that fully 60 percent of its students are youth and special-needs participants. Enviable, too, are the breadth and depth of the activities offered; these include hillwalking and camping, rock climbing, sailing, and canoeing.

The school is confident and looks to the future with optimism. Derek Pritchard, the school's executive director, definitively states: "Fundamental to Outward Bound Hong Kong's future is a belief that the qualities that an Outward Bound course engenders will see us through the exciting challenges which surely lie ahead."

Given limited time and materials with which to construct a raft, these Hong Kong students paddle to base camp in the hills near Sai Kung.

Overlooking the pastoral serenity of Tai Mong Tsai, these students seem far removed from the bustling city centre only a few miles away.

*Making use of the natural challenge of nearby mountains, instructors
guide their students through intense and often exhausting activities.*

Outward Bound Hong Kong

A Hong Kong crew anchors for the first time in the distant and unfamiliar waters of the Philippines.

PHOTOGRAPH: JOHN GRENDON

The majestic brigantine **Ji Fung,** *"The Spirit of Resolution," sets sail on a 22-day voyage bound for the Philippines.*

By facing difficult physical challenges and pulling together in teamwork, students are empowered to reach towards their potential.

Sea kayakers ride undulating swells from island to island in Hong Kong's inner harbour.

"I thought that I was ordinary, and I was satisfied with a standard below my ability. But, here, I was not allowed such self-indulgence. I continued to tell myself that I could do more and more . . . and I could."

Humbled by the barren icescape of Canada's frozen north, sled teams follow skiers across the vast expanse of Frobisher Bay. The Canadian Outward Bound Wilderness School runs Arctic expeditions every spring when conditions are less hostile.

North America

Fact: Its ropes course, including a 300-foot zip wire, is suspended a meaningful 80 feet above the deck of the four-masted brigantine *Peking*, berthed at the South Street Seaport. Fact: Its water-based activities may involve boating on the East River and New York Harbour. Fact: Camp-outs may be held at the base of skyscrapers and rock-climbs below the Cloisters in Fort Tryon State Park. Fact: One of its challenges is to provide dinner for 12 with $20 in one of the world's most expensive cities.

What is it? The sixth and most recent facility founded in the United States: the NEW YORK CITY OUTWARD BOUND CENTER. Launched in 1987, it is the only independently chartered urban centre in the world.

Its primary mission is to make a difference in the lives of New York City youth of all backgrounds by using Outward Bound content and methodology. One way to do this is to go right into the schools. For a minimum of one semester, specially trained Outward Bound staff work with New York City teachers and their students to integrate Outward Bound programmes with prescribed curricula. After school and on weekends, adventure activities in the form of climbing, canoeing, backpacking, and community service projects are also introduced.

A second programme pairs young people from the city's schools and various community-based organisations with committed adults in a series of adventure and community service experiences. The adults are often representatives and mentors from the city's business community. Course participants come away with a renewed appreciation for New York and its diversity while often a unique bonding occurs between young people and adults who seemingly had little in common.

Community service for the disadvantaged and elderly nurtures compassion and sensitivity in the city core. Here, volunteers lend a hand in a soup kitchen for homeless people.

PHOTOGRAPH: JOHN ALLISON

Outward Bound programmes were once conducted exclusively in the wilderness. New York City's Outward Bound Center transfers the same principles of leadership and self-reliance to an urban setting.

PHOTOGRAPH: EDI JURICIC

Hanging from the yardarm above the South Street Seaport, students negotiate the ropes course high in the rigging of The Peking.

PHOTOGRAPH: BRENDA WALKER

A crew from the Hurricane Island Outward Bound School navigates in Penobscot Bay, one of the last remaining United States coastal wilderness areas.

Paddlers in sleek double-kayaks explore islands and inlets ten miles off the coast of Maine.

*Abandoned by their instructor on a remote island for a "shipwreck" exercise,
teammates are drawn closer together while stranded overnight.*

It takes compassion and commitment to be an Outward Bound instructor. Facing a personal crisis, a troubled teenager is counselled by a group leader at Hurricane Island's land base in Maine.

Young students on a Youth at Risk programme gather in the Florida Keys. Discovering that the past need not equal the future can alter the direction of their lives.

Basic in its design, the spritsail ketch is a rugged and versatile craft. "You can take 'em anywhere," claims the school director at Big Pine Key.

113

On sailing expeditions crew members have an opportunity to snorkel in the coral reefs south of Florida, where marine life abounds.

"Outward Bound transcends class and individual differences and kindles within each of us a sense of community and a strong dedication to service. The wilderness environment allows one's veneers to slip away and each person can grow through daring to risk, to care, and to share with others. As an educational forum, Outward Bound offers true learning, involving heart, mind, and body in a way that will last a lifetime."

The NORTH CAROLINA OUTWARD BOUND SCHOOL, the third mountain and last wilderness school established in the United States, is acknowledged to have the best rock climbing and the "highest, toughest, scariest" ropes course in the country. Special sources of pride are emphases on a commitment to service and on personal growth and human relations.

Its first and principal site lies at the end of a dirt road on a hillside under Table Rock Mountain. This 80-acre base camp is leased from the U.S. Forest Service near Morganton, in western North Carolina. The setting is most felicitous: spectacular rock faces in natural forested areas, paddling rivers, and mountain camps are all conveniently accessible.

Also on the site is the Kurt Hahn Leadership Center, a separate facility, which annually trains more than 300 students in experiential educational techniques and methodology. The Center spreads the mission of Outward Bound by raising standards of safety and quality throughout the field of outdoor experiential education.

Today there are two different base camps in the Appalachian and Smoky mountains, covering almost 300 acres and accommodating 264 students, and a third on an island in the Florida Everglades, complete with a 1920s resort, housing 72. North Carolina students might also be found on Outward Bound projects in Tennessee and Georgia and as far afield as Costa Rica and Mexico.

Winter mist envelops the southern Appalachians, where hikers stop to catch their breath near Grandfather Mountain.

PHOTOGRAPH: BARRY ROSEN

Fifteen-year-old hikers from the North Carolina Outward Bound School contend with swamp and dense sawgrass in Florida's Everglades, a unique and threatened ecosystem.

118

Timing their movements according to tides, students navigate the Everglades' labyrinth of mangrove tunnels, which sustains a huge variety of exotic wildlife.

The North Carolina Outward Bound School uses some of the best climb sites in the eastern United States. Here, a senior student throws a belay rope to waiting climbers below.

120

The Chattooga, a wild and scenic river bordering Georgia and South
Carolina, carries expeditions into the heartland of the South.

Service is one of the four pillars of Kurt Hahn's philosophy. Offering companionship and support, students from Green Cove base camp help an elderly neighbour to clear her fields.

*The ropes course at Table Rock base, a dramatic arena for confronting
fear and taking action, features a maze of events rising 65 feet.*

PHOTOGRAPH: BARRY ROSEN

Canoe expeditions can be anticipated at the VOYAGEUR OUTWARD BOUND SCHOOL, given the fact that "les voyageurs" were 18th-century French fur trappers and traders who plied the "Land of 10,000 Lakes" by birchbark canoe.

"Homeplace," the school's base camp, is ideally situated on the doorstep of Superior National Forest, close to Canada's Quetico Provincial Park. Voyageur Outward Bound School also runs mobile courses from leased bases in the Beartooth Mountains of Montana and on the Rio Grande River in Texas. In addition, for the last five years urban programmes, in Chicago and Minneapolis/St. Paul (the first urban programme in the United States), have been a major focus of the school.

After but one year of operation, school director Bob Pieh turned some heads in the United States Outward Bound world by announcing the offer of all-women's courses in 1965. Controversy reigned, media coverage was assured, success was proclaimed, and the next year four times the original number of women became Outward Bound alumnae. The logical extension was coeducational courses that were rapidly adopted by the other United States schools. Hard on the heels of this triumph, the next director, Alan Hale, pioneered the concept of winter courses, an awesome undertaking given the area's challenging weather conditions. Once again in the forefront, Voyageur Outward Bound School named Nan Skelton, a former Minnesota Assistant Commissioner of Education, as its Executive Director. She is the first woman to serve in this capacity in the United States.

Regardless of season and course activities, however, Voyageur Outward Bound School emphasises the beauty and fragility of nature and fosters humanistic relationships. Challenge, including "controlled understandable stress," is certainly a part of Voyageur's experience, but process, too, is important.

On a Life Renewal course at Voyageur's Minnesota base, a 65-year-old student reaches out to grasp "monkey fists" to steady her advance across a suspended wire.

A student, swinging like a pendulum in a giant arc above the ground, is harnessed to "The Breathtaker," the last obstacle on the high ropes course.

In contrast to the inexperienced crew who embarked on expedition three weeks earlier, these seasoned paddlers push homeward with new skills, new strengths, and newfound friends.

Portaging is difficult and tiring, but it is necessary in order to traverse northern Minnesota's vast wilderness of lakes, rivers, and forests.

Kayakers practise capsize and self-rescue drills before facing white-water rapids.

Their energy spent from an exhausting trek through Montana's Beartooth Range, hikers seek relief in the icy waters of a mountain lake.

Surrounded by the bleak Chihuahuan Desert, kayakers round "The Anvil" on the Rio Grande River in southwest Texas.

"As a young Huckleberry Finn, barefoot and free to explore, I knew the joys of outdoor roaming. When I fell in with the Minnesota Outward Bound School, I knew in that summer of 1965 that somehow I was home again. I learned firsthand that an Outward Bound course opens people up to learning in a most remarkable way. I see Outward Bound as a leader and catalyst for human dignity, peace, and racial and ethnic understanding. The beautiful thing about belonging to the Outward Bound community is that you feel connected to other wildly idealistic mavericks and professional vagabonds all over the world. It keeps you in touch with the mud squishing between your toes and the beauty of the stars — as if one could just keep right on being Huckleberry Finn and never grow old."

The COLORADO OUTWARD BOUND SCHOOL, the first Outward Bound school in the Western Hemisphere, was founded in the Colorado Rockies in 1961. From the outset the U.S.-U.K. connection was strong, so it was logical that the first courses offered in the summer of 1962 should be quite similar to the Eskdale mountain model. But from practically the beginning, two innovations were introduced. The first was a marked predilection for mobile courses, and the second involved a longer, more meaningful solo.

On the occasion of Colorado Outward Bound School's celebration of its 25th anniversary, two events occurred that emphasised the timelessness of this U.S.-U.K. connection: a 13,420-foot mountain in Colorado's Maroon Bells/Snowmass area was named Kurt Hahn Peak, and the Duke of Edinburgh was invited to Denver to receive the Kurt Hahn Award "in appreciation for outstanding service to the furthering of the Outward Bound mission around the world."

Today, the Colorado Outward Bound School runs more than 200 year-round courses featuring Alpine mountaineering, white-water rafting, horsetrailing, ski-mountaineering and cross-country skiing, desert canyoneering, hiking and backpacking, sport yakking, and several multi-environment experiences. They are run in eight mountain areas in Colorado, Utah, California, Arizona, on a number of western United States rivers, and in far-flung U.S.S.R., Nepal, Alaska, and Argentina. The school is also actively assisting Eastern Bloc countries with their Outward Bound futures, the primary result of courses run for the last four years with a mix of Hungarian, Soviet, and American students.

High in the Rockies, courses range from short cross-country clinics to 18 days of intense ski-mountaineering at Colorado's Leadville base.

Like many United States schools, the Colorado Outward Bound School has created special programs for Vietnam veterans, cancer survivors, drug addicts, and victims of violence.

*A peaceful respite between rapids allows raft teams to enjoy the beauty
of sandstone formations in Lodore Canyon.*

Having studied the rapids from shore, students run "Hell's Half Mile," named by John Wesley Powell during his famed expedition in 1869.

Crew members alternate as captain, making split-second decisions and reading the river as it unfolds before them.

Most of us have far greater potential than we dare to explore. Setting new limits for themselves and surpassing them, students re-define what is possible.

In the frontier spirit of the Old West, a horseback expedition follows a stretch of the Outlaw Trail in northern Utah.

"The purpose of the course is not to conquer nature, but to cooperate with it and learn about it. That's when you find out that 'natural resources' refers to you, too."

The PACIFIC CREST OUTWARD BOUND SCHOOL, founded in 1966, the fourth in the U.S., has run all mobile courses since its inception. A seminal statement of the time was that "training is conducted on the trail, with the emphasis on learning by doing." This concept proved to be one of the most far-reaching innovations of the United States Outward Bound movement.

This school's wilderness is singularly wild. Its rivers, peaks, glaciers, and canyons are spread along the Pacific Crest Trail. In Washington, students climb the North Cascades or trek along the Olympic National Seashore, the longest stretch of roadless coastline in the United States. In Oregon, students go white-water rafting and hike among dormant volcanoes and across glaciers in the Central Cascades, where terrain varies from heavily forested mountain slopes to sagebrush country. And in California, participants trek along the highest mountain range on the West Coast, the southern Sierras, or go hiking or rock climbing in Joshua Tree National Monument, where boulders the size of houses offer spectacular climbs.

Other facts make Pacific Crest Outward Bound School unique: its course areas are among the most remote and challenging in the United States; its instructional staff is particularly technically skilled, but is also noted for its teamwork and creativity; and the school makes a concerted commitment to community service, notably in the areas of mountain rescue, fire fighting, and trail building and maintenance.

In Joshua Tree National Monument, teams become immersed in the
alien environment of California's high desert.

Climbers must rely on each other and work together as a unit to conquer Twin Peaks in the southern Sierra mountains.

*Days of hiking are long and hard in Sequoia National Park. Exhausted
yet elated, a student experiences a sense of real accomplishment.*

144

As navigation and other essential wilderness skills are mastered, students take turns leading the team on expedition.

The North Sister, a dormant volcano, looms majestically beyond a lava field in central Oregon. Natural history and environmental protection are an integral part of courses at the Pacific Crest Outward Bound School.

Unique, perhaps, in Outward Bound history, one day in April 1988, OUTWARD BOUND WESTERN CANADA (then Outward Bound British Columbia) moved its 19-year site ten hours distant and radically changed direction and scope in a single stroke. To realise capital and extricate itself from a "wilderness" area that was becoming increasingly overcrowded, it sold its 184-acre site and went mobile, concentrating on people rather than facilities. In fact, the new location two hours north of Vancouver in the population-700-village of Pemberton had been the runner-up choice when a site was first selected in 1969.

Outward Bound Western Canada's new logistical facility is located near Whistler in the Coast Range of British Columbia and the dramatic Lillooet Ice Fields, an unspoilt Alpine wilderness area that still provides easy access via logging roads. Set in a long, one and a half kilometre-wide agricultural valley and surrounded by mountain peaks rising to 2,800 metres, Pemberbase, as it is known, offers rugged terrain, mountain snow into July (and year-round on glaciers), and little backcountry use.

All Western Canada's courses are mobile and are supported from this base. The focus is mountaineering. Climbing, hiking, and the solo are major activities; in winter, ski-mountaineering and cross-country skiing replace hiking, while the solo experience may find participants sleeping in snow caves and tents at high altitudes.

For almost 15 years, since the Wilderness School in Ontario was established as the second Canadian Outward Bound centre, the two schools have remained virtually totally independent. Now, however, Outward Bound Canada has been founded to administer both schools. One of its first commitments will be national fund-raising strategies toward the establishment of a substantial endowment fund.

To witness the majesty of a soaring eagle is a unique reward for students on mobile courses in British Columbia's Coast Mountains.

Shouldering heavy backpacks across steep slopes of rugged terrain, students at Outward Bound Western Canada develop strength and stamina.

Instructors must possess special mountaineering skills, experience, and expertise in order to create new climb and rappel sites in deep backcountry.

It is unlikely that students will encounter other human beings on their trek into 600 square kilometres of incredible alpine wilderness.

PHOTOGRAPH: OUTWARD BOUND WESTERN CANADA

As a student gazes into the mouth of a vast glacial cave, he seems dwarfed in a landscape of giant proportions.

PHOTOGRAPH: ROTH HALL

"(This experience) helped me recognise strengths, both physical and emotional, within myself. It was also an aesthetic experience in relishing the beauty of the environment."

The CANADIAN OUTWARD BOUND WILDERNESS SCHOOL is aptly named. With access only by seaplane, canoe, or rough dirt logging road, its 25-acre site is the lone outpost on Black Sturgeon Lake, 100 miles north of Thunder Bay in northern Ontario and 45 miles from any settlement. Without question, it is the most isolated of all Outward Bound centres.

Its cluster of buildings, known as Homeplace and including housing for more than 50 staff members, is set in a thickly wooded forest of spruce and balsam fir; vertical bluffs and rushing mountain streams dominate the landscape beyond the lake's shore.

Incongruously, perhaps, courses are run year-round. In summer, canoeing and portaging, white-water kayaking, rock climbing, and hiking are featured. A solo experience of two to three days is sited in a forested wilderness. Winter, which finds 336 centimetres of snow cover in an average season, provides cross-country skiing, snowshoeing, and dogsledding, including the opportunity to work with and care for teams of huskies. In recent years, Baffin Island in the Arctic has proved an intriguing springtime destination. The centre also runs a number of directive programmes, targeting very specific participants.

The Wilderness School is particularly proud of its reputation as a school with a strong community focus. Its mission is forcefully delineated: "To promote self-reliance, care and respect for others, responsibility to the community, and concern for the environment."

An instructor demonstrates white-water kayak manoeuvres on a churning section of the Black Sturgeon River, affectionately known as "The Washing Machine."

Students rappelling from Claghorn enjoy a magnificent view of northern Ontario's boreal forest.

The Canadian Outward Bound Wilderness School is one of the most remote of the world's centres. At Homeplace a group plots its final winter expedition.

In the silver dawn, the marathon begins. Students develop strength and endurance, combining new skills to complete the demanding course — paddling, portaging, and finally, long-distance running.

A local Inuit develops a strong rapport with sled dogs and fellow students from across Canada on a bicultural course in the Northwest Territories.

Forerunners of the snowmobile, Alaskan huskies pull komatiks laden with equipment and supplies over the frozen landscape of Baffin Island.

After hiking to the top of a fjord, students enjoy a panorama of Frobisher Bay at sunset.

In the semi-darkness of a spring Arctic night, an expedition sleeps. Soon students will awake to the splendour of a northern sunrise.

"The trick is not to rid your stomach of butterflies but to make them fly in formation."

Early morning light bathes hikers crossing the Bundi Plain.

Africa

OUTWARD BOUND ZIMBABWE, located in the Chimanimani Mountain National Park, has two histories. From its establishment in 1961, it had an excellent multi-racial record, flourishing for 15 years in its remote and magnificent mountain setting, but then the politics of the time and place caught up with it. Rhodesian sanctions, guerilla raids on the area, and security problems in general forced its closure in 1977.

More than five years later, given a much more stable political environment, it was thought feasible to re-activate the centre. Assisted initially by instructors and staff from Ullswater and Rhowniar, the centre was re-opened in February 1987, a full ten years after its demise.

Since its reincarnation, it can make several dramatic claims. The Outward Bound Zimbabwe centre, with no more than 500 participants per year, is possibly the smallest in the world operating year-round. It also prides itself on being self-supporting. Although it was initially staffed by at least three consecutive British Outward Bound instructors, now Zimbabweans lead the centre. It proudly states that while it was one of the earliest fully multi-racial organisations in the country during its previous operating period, it is now once again taking the lead in this area and is actively encouraging international participation.

Two histories is all that Outward Bound Zimbabwe wants, and its current one will be further assured with its plans to promote new family and mobile courses and to nurture qualified staff from enthusiastic ex-students.

After a progression of climbs leading to the ultimate challenge of "The Sphinx," students abseil the 85-metre rock face.

Guiding a teammate through the centre of the "Spider Web" is difficult without touching the ropes.

Students awake to the inspiring view of a mountain in Mozambique
that they will ascend before nightfall.

Think of Kenya and images of Mt. Kilimanjaro come to mind. The OUTWARD BOUND MOUNTAIN SCHOOL (EAST AFRICA) was established here in 1952 at 5,500 feet on the north flank of Kilimanjaro in order to put Kenyan, Tanzanian, and Ugandan boys on the summit of the mountain. In fact, course descriptions from the mid-'50s detail "one of the most demanding of expeditions in any Outward Bound school." Most of the curriculum involved preparation and training for the ascent: the ultimate goal — Kaiser Wilhelm Spitz at 19,300 feet.

But then, as today, the school's greater purpose was to prepare young men, and subsequently women, to assume positions of responsible leadership in a developing country. Entirely Kenyan-run since 1976, the school continues to bring African, Asian, European, and other Western students together for courses that promote harmony between races, ethnic groups, and nations. A non-profit Trust in Nairobi now supervises courses with a greater variety of everything: duration, activities, sites, curricula, and participant backgrounds. The Trust enjoys support from industry, schools, and the government, with much of the teaching staff seconded by the Ministry of Education.

250 miles southeast of the administrative office in Nairobi is the base camp at Loitokitok, a 40-acre site of forest and farmland. Half a participant's time is spent here on activities very similar to those of the boy-patrols 35 years earlier. But the time spent on expedition "in the field" finds patrols not only on Kilimanjaro, but also on Mt. Kenya, in the high desert country of the Rift Valley, and in various of the safari parks in the area.

In training for the Kenya Armed Forces, an officer cadet scales the sheer face of Rhino Rock.

PHOTGRAPH: STEVE McCORMICK

A class at Loitokitok watches intently as the instructor demonstrates the various knots to be mastered before climbing Africa's highest peak, Mt. Kilimanjaro.

PHOTOGRAPH: STEVE McCORMICK

From its start OUTWARD BOUND LESOTHO has been ahead of its time and place. It was established in 1974 in northwest Lesotho, a country ruled by King Moshoeshoe II that is completely surrounded by South Africa. It was founded essentially to bring together the people of southern Africa and to provide non-racial understanding, respect, and concern. It has simply ignored apartheid and has always been multi-racial. In fact, a large majority of its clients are from South Africa, the staff is being called upon to conduct more and more social development courses, and the time now seems appropriate to expand activities into South Africa itself.

Outward Bound Lesotho's setting supports its quite remarkable course variety. Located in the Maloti Mountains at Thaba Phatsoa in the Leribe district of Lesotho at 5,400 feet, it occupies 35 hectares above a small lake on a rocky hillside topped with sandstone cliffs. It is essentially a mountain school, with all the activities that this implies (including a 200-foot abseil), but nearby lakes and rivers permit sailing and canoeing, too.

Two quite out-of-the-ordinary occurrences may make up part of a group's course experience. First, more use is being made of the area's local Basotho ponies; two-week pony treks are being considered, and the centre is earning an increasing reputation for its horseback riding speciality. Second, seven- to eight-day hiking expeditions find participants using villagers' huts for overnight accommodation; the villagers eagerly welcome their Outward Bound guests.

An instructor from a local village calms a frightened abseiler on the "Great Slab."

The stark grandeur of the Black and White Mountains form the backdrop for kayakers on the small lake near Outward Bound Lesotho.

Reaching a crucial stage of the exercise, a student struggles to maintain control on the crossover ropes.

The Basotho pony, a breed unique to this region, is known for stamina and agility in mountainous terrain. Riders learn about tack and saddlery before setting off on expedition.

Using the traditional method of travel, strangers from Outward Bound Lesotho are welcomed in villages dotting the Maloti Mountains.

Lesotho is the homeland of the proud Basotho people. A cultural interface develops between students from urban South Africa and this gentle race.

An expedition winds along a bridle path formerly used to carry grain and supplies by donkey up to White Man's Pass, named for the Europeans who constructed the trail 70 years ago.

Predjudices and preconceived social norms are abandoned in an environment where participants share together all aspects of living.

"I've convinced myself that no matter how close I feel I am to my limits, physically or mentally, I'm still an enormous distance away."

At present, the TANZANIAN OUTWARD BOUND CENTRE consists of a temporary building and several tents. There was more, and, with assistance and work, there will be more again.

In 1979 the border between Tanzania and Kenya was closed. One ramification of the closure was that Tanzanians no longer had access to the Outward Bound Centre Mountain School (East Africa) across the border in Loitokitok, Kenya. Thus, Tanzania's own centre at Marangu at 6,100 feet on the southeastern slopes of Mt. Kilimanjaro was born. The first three to four years of the centre's existence were quite successful. Since 1982, however, the number of courses declined until there were simply no courses at all.

In 1988 and 1989 chance meetings between the warden of the centre, Outward Bound U.S.A. trustees, and staff of the Outward Bound Mountain School in Loitokitok revealed that, while operating on a shoestring budget with none of its own equipment or transport, Outward Bound Tanzania was nonetheless still operating. The centre could still state that it was "open to all people, regardless of race, religion, or education" and that it endeavoured to teach basic skills and pursue a number of activities.

This chance encounter, in fact, prompted that earnest statement and provided the first-hand evidence that a great deal was needed by the centre if it was to continue to survive. Cooperation has been pledged from several quarters. The future of Outward Bound Tanzania, though still ultimately uncertain, has at least been extended.

"Outward Bound is just great. What if half of the world's population was to 'set sail' on this adventure! What a peaceful, friendly, and harmonious people we would be!"

Zambia's OUTWARD BOUND LAKE SCHOOL in Mbala is a great deal more than an outdoor education centre. It is a community whose goal is nothing short of self-sufficiency.

Its 713 acres of thick bushland, originally the site of a coffee plantation and subsequently the buildings and grounds of the Lake View Hotel, have been cleared. A working farm to provide the centre with its own meat and vegetables has also been established. A herd of cattle supplies dairy products, and a fish hatchery supplements the community's diet. The teaching of agricultural methods is in fact part of the centre's course curriculum. A primary school and clinic for the local population are also on the site, and it has its own electricity and spring water supplies. Other facilities include a workshop, football ground, volleyball pitch, and swimming pool.

At 5,500 feet above sea level, near the southern end of Lake Tanganyika, it is most fortunate in its setting and its wide variety of activities. Surrounded by mountainous terrain and covered with thick African bush, the site supports lake activities such as canoeing, sailing, and rafting, utilises the bush for hiking expeditions, and looks to the mountains for rock climbing and abseiling. In short, the combination of these natural elements offers an ideal environment for Outward Bound training. Various community service projects connected with the centre's self-sufficiency goal, map reading, first aid, two ropes courses, and the solo experience round out the curriculum.

"Outward Bound shows you where to look — inside yourself."

Students roller-skating by the River Maas are silhouetted against the Rotterdam skyline. Dutch City Bound courses combine physical challenge with practical career training and job-search skills.

Europe

The beginnings of OUTWARD BOUND NETHERLANDS were quite prosaic. After Germany, the Netherlands was the second European country to found an Outward Bound centre. In 1960-61 a sea school was established on the Dutch coast in the southwest delta; its first staff travelled to Aberdovey for training; its first trainees were working youth, students, and company executives.

Times, however, change. Partial compulsory education for 16- to 19-year-olds was introduced, chronic unemployment became quite widespread, and the practical education of young seamen was considered a priority. In each instance, Outward Bound Netherlands was at the forefront, participating in and formulating new programmes for a wide range of needs.

It is Outward Bound Netherlands' social programmes and concerns and its close association with the Ministry of Education in the areas of funding and initiative that have made it a model for other far-reaching international programmes. Concentrating on young school-leavers and the long-term unemployed, Outward Bound Netherlands recognised that more emphasis should be placed on discussions and follow-up after adventure activities, and so it introduced a new group dynamic in its courses.

With the urbanisation of more and more of its potential clientele, Outward Bound Netherlands formulated the City Bound concept in 1983. Using the city as a resource and working closely with job centres and potential employers, City Bound trainees learn practical skills and more about themselves and their own potential from structured urban experiences, their group leaders, and each other.

An Outward Bound programme in France for the long-term unemployed introduces tough physical demands that can bring raw emotions to the surface.

Rather than dwelling on seemingly insurmountable barriers, students are encouraged to re-direct their energies into achieving positive results.

Having returned to Rotterdam's City Bound base, students complete intensive career profiles before immersing themselves in the job-search process.

Actively involving the group in labour market research, interviews with workers from a variety of businesses are captured on videotape for debriefing.

Caving and climbing techniques are introduced at an abandoned army bunker on the island of Pampus. This Pre-Sea Training course crew lives on a renovated river barge, moving within the IJsselmeer, the Netherlands' inland sea.

A fire-fighting team combats a towering pillar of flame at a specially equipped base near Lelystad Harbour.

The school ship Outward Bound *looms like an apparition on the IJsselmeer, where crews have spent 24 hours afloat on a rescue dinghy.*

"The course has been a reminder that life can be simpler, that problems can be surmounted, that nature is majestic, and that strangers can become friends."

A capsule history of OUTWARD BOUND GERMANY reveals that the country's first mountain school at BAAD, technically in Austria but with access only from Germany, first welcomed students in 1956. 1969 saw Outward Bound BERCHTESGADEN, a second mountain school, established. And in 1988 Outward Bound KONIGSBURG, situated on a peninsula on the banks of the Schlei fjord, became Germany's new sea centre.

Baad and Berchtesgaden have several significant things in common. Both run mountaineering courses in the high Alps, and the state has mandated that certified mountain guides must accompany all expeditions. In addition, because the "inward" experience is at least as important as "outward" activities, facilitators well-versed in pedagogy also work with each student group. Summertime activities include walking, trekking, and climbing, along with white-water rafting (Baad) and kayaking (Berchtesgaden); in winter cross-country and Alpine skiing are featured.

Both areas encourage reflection and feedback and also provide important opportunities for ecological and community/social projects, and musical and other creative outlets. Virtually all course offerings at both Baad and Berchtesgaden are centre-based, though one- to three-day mobile courses are also provided.

Ecology and environmental protection concerns in part prompted the founding of Germany's new sea school at Konigsburg. Ecological projects like water investigation, environmental problems, wildlife conservation, and nature management have been chosen as a special focus of Konigsburg for youth and adult teams alike; this, of course, is in addition to the school's emphasis on sailing and other water-based activities. A number of ambitious mobile courses are planned involving cutter and jolly boat sailing, bicycling, kayaking, and excursions throughout the Baltic, including Denmark and Finland.

Various habitats of northern Germany become an open-air laboratory for ecology projects at Outward Bound Konigsburg. Learning by doing, students develop greater sensitivity and understanding of the natural environment.

193

Outward Bound Konigsburg

Hoisting multi-coloured sails, corporate trainees cross the Schlei en route to their expedition on the Baltic Sea.

Students provide community service by constructing a walkway over wetlands leading to the school jetty.

Teamwork and cooperation are required to pedal tandem cycles on expedition through rural villages and rolling hills of the German countryside.

Outward Bound Berchtesgaden

Courses from the Alpine lodge at Outward Bound Berchtesgaden
begin with students "jumping into a new life" on the "Flying Fox."

Students use ropes to descend the slippery trail on Rauherkopf "Hard
Hat", which overlooks a picturesque village in southeast Bavaria.

Individuals work in synergy to negotiate strong currents in the
Saalach River on the Austro-German border.

1,230 metres above sea level in Austria's Kleinwalsertal, superb snow conditions create the perfect venue for ski touring, cross-country, and Alpine expeditions at Outward Bound Baad.

PHOTOGRAPH: BERND HECKMAIR

Groups summon newly acquired skills and ingenuity to cross a deep river gorge, the final hurdle of an arduous mountaineering expedition.

"Outward Bound has given me a rare opportunity to look at myself both mentally and physically and to find weaknesses and strengths that I didn't know I possessed. I've come away from the course with a better understanding of myself and my potential."

"Small but choice" would be an apt description of the BELGIUM OUTWARD BOUND SCHOOL.

From the start, it was a joint venture linking educational interests and concerns in physical education and sports psychology with leading business organisations. The result was foreshortened "Standard" courses of five to seven days and executive training courses of four to five days. Mobile courses in the Spanish Pyrenees and French Verdon are run for 10 to 14 days on average.

Actually, "Standard" courses have never really existed. Trainers, who are hired and extensively trained for both their "hard" and "soft" skill expertise, do not follow a fixed programme. Each group's course is drawn up while in progress and takes specific group characteristics and processes fully into account. On any course major attention goes to process facilitation and communication between participants and trainers.

The school's present base is a country house located in the Belgian Ardennes, to which it moved in 1980. It is set amongst a landscape of forests and fields near the River Meuse and its tributaries. Accommodation is provided for three groups of ten each, with rental lodging available nearby for another 40 participants. The groups may work totally independently, but common activities include hillwalking, rock climbing, rafting and canoeing, camping, and caving. In addition to this variety, participants are responsible for their own cooking and the maintenance of their accommodation.

In the Ardennes, a pastoral region of forests, rivers, and rocky hillsides, a human chain ascends de schuine helling ("the steep slope").

Belgian Outward Bound School students climb while blindfolded, which improves communication and trust among teammates who verbally guide each other along the rock face.

203

One by one, students walk in solitude through the Ravin du Colebi,
Belgium's last remaining wilderness.

Beyond the stately Chateau de Freyr an expedition traverses the River
Meuse around seemingly impassable cliffs in southern Belgium.

Emotions run high and reactions vary dramatically when fear of an activity, or fear itself, triggers an outburst. Caring and compassion from within the group provide comfort in a moment of anguish.

"Outward Bound as a metaphor means to me the ever-repeating transition from static to dynamic during a person's lifetime. Its code word is *Aufbruch* 'a breaking out or awakening'. Its fascinating task is to help people to go ahead into no-man's land, which might be at any period of life. Outward Bound leads to a mental attitude that protects us from the danger and temptations of the modern world by mobilising physical and mental strengths, and, at the same time, that prepares the individual to face the unexpected and exceptional in his own future."

In the early 1980s Alain Kerjean, the French traveller, explorer, writer, and television producer, made a documentary film on the centre at Aberdovey, Wales. So enthusiastic was he about all he witnessed that he became the driving force for the establishment of the first Outward Bound centre in France, indeed in any Latin country, HORS LIMITES OUTWARD BOUND FRANCE.

The statement of Outward Bound International that "each new school must adapt and develop in order to suit its particular cultural and environmental circumstances while remaining true to the Outward Bound philosophy" can be applied most aptly to France. Here it is felt that this brings up to date the philosophical movement of Jean-Jacques Rousseau, "the master of New Education," which was born in France a century ago. Following closely, too, the Netherlands' and Belgium's concept of Outward Bound, no absolutely fixed programme is presented. "L'aventure vous revele" is Outward Bound France's motto; self-evaluation and conceptualisation are the keys.

To date, all this has been accomplished in rented accommodation and facilities two hours north of Nice in a small village in the southern Alps near an area of mountains, lakes and rivers, and prehistoric caves. A full complement of activities can be enjoyed, including climbing and abseiling, caving, kayaking, canoeing, rafting, orienteering, and various dynamics experiences. Hors Limites Outward Bound France is currently establishing its first permanent base camp in the department of Lozere, in southern France.

A group of inner-city youth plan their route through the dense, thorny undergrowth of the Verdon — challenging terrain for teenagers accustomed to life in the back streets of Paris.

Participants come to Hors Limites Outward Bound with preconceived goals shaped by the daily trials of private life. The byproduct of extraordinary achievement is often a startling new perspective.

In the intricate maze of tunnels in La Grotte des Fees, students crawl 400 metres through dank, narrow passageways to find their way out of the labyrinth.

Twilight falls around a cave entrance where students prepare their evening meal, conjuring images of a prehistoric age when Cro-Magnon man inhabited this cavernous region of southern France.

As the sun sets in the Verdon, a young student reflects upon the first day of his Outward Bound course. Through the trials and triumphs of the weeks ahead he hopes to discover a new sense of self-worth and achievement, compassion, and service to others.

INTERNATIONAL SECRETARIAT

Outward Bound Trust Ltd.
Chestnut Field, Regent Place
Rugby, Warwickshire CV21 2PJ England
Telephone: (44) 788 560423
Fax: (44) 788 541069

AFFILIATE MEMBERS

AUSTRALIA

Australian Outward Bound Foundation
GPO Box 4213
Sydney, NSW 2001
Chairman: Carlo Bongarzoni
Exec. Director: Garry E. Richards
Telephone: (61) 2 261 2200
Fax: (61) 2 261 3475

Australian Outward Bound National Base
c/o Post Office, Tharwa
ACT 2620
Director: Garry E. Richards
Associate Director: Allan Riches
Telephone: (61) 6 237 5158
Fax: (61) 6 237 5224

BELGIUM

Outward Bound School Belgie
Kapucijnenvoer 217
3000 Leuven
Director: Yves Verraes
Telephone: (32) 16 23 51 72
Fax: (32) 16 29 03 09

CANADA

Outward Bound Western Canada
1367 West Broadway
Vancouver, British Columbia V6H 4A9
Exec. Director: Andrew Orr
Telephone: (1) 604 737 3093
Fax: (1) 604 738 7175

Canadian Outward Bound Wilderness School
P.O. Box 116, Station "S"
Toronto, Ontario M5M 4L6
Exec. Director: Philip Blackford
Telephone: (1) 416 787 1721
Fax: (1) 416 787 7335

Outward Bound Canada
250 Ferrand Drive, 15th Floor
Don Mills, Ontario M3C 3J4
Director of Development: Frances Sommerville
Telephone: (1) 416 424 5209
Fax: (1) 416 424 1008

FRANCE

Hors Limites Outward Bound
76 rue d'Anjou
78000 Versailles
President: Alain Kerjean
Telephone: (33) 1 39 50 68 00
Fax: (33) 1 39 50 03 47

GERMANY

Outward Bound Deutsche Gesellschaft fur
   Europaische Erziehung e.V.
Nymphenburger Strasse 42
D-8000 Munchen 2
Director: Rainer Guttler
Telephone: (49) 89 18 10 58
Fax: (49) 89 18 39 33

Outward Bound Kurzschule Berchtesgaden
Locksteinstrasse 49
D-8240 Berchtesgaden
Warden: Georg Samhuber
Telephone: (49) 86 52 4094
Fax: (49) 86 52 5520

Outward Bound Kurzschule Baad
Kleinwalsertal
D-8986 Mittelberg Baad
Warden: Gustav Harder
Telephone: (49) 83 29 5042
Fax: (49) 83 29 3480

Outward Bound Sea School Konigsburg
D-2332 Bohnert/Kosel
Warden: Rainer Stange
Telephone: (49) 4355 268

HONG KONG

Outward Bound Hong Kong
Tai Mong Tsai
Sai Kung
New Territories
Kowloon
Exec. Director: Derek Pritchard
Telephone: (852) 792 4333
Fax: (852) 792 9877

JAPAN

Outward Bound Japan (Headquarters)
301 Silver Hill
2-12 Shirogane-cho
Shinjuku-Ku
Tokyo 162
Warden: Takeshi Kitani
Telephone: (81) 3 3235 - 5757
Fax: (81) 3 3267 - 6023
Outward Bound Japan Nagano School
Oami, Kita Otari
Otari Village, Kita Azumi-Gun
Nagano Prefecture 399-96
Telephone: (81) 255 572211

Outward Bound Japan (International Division)
Sanno Grand Building, Rm. 422
14-2, Nagata-cho 2 Chome
Chiyoda-Ku Tokyo 100
Chairman: Koichi Inasawa
Telephone: (81) 3 3580 - 3451
Fax: (81) 3 3581 - 3633

KENYA

Outward Bound Trust of Kenya
P.O. Box 49576
#7 Kenya Cultural Centre
Nairobi
Exec. Director: James Oswago
Telephone: (254) 2 28764

Outward Bound Mountain School
P.O. Box 10
Loitokitok
Program Director: Steve McCormick
Telephone: 58

LESOTHO

Outward Bound Association of Lesotho/
   Southern Africa
P.O. Box 346
Ficksburg
Republic of South Africa
Exec. Director: Roger Binns
Telephone: (27) 563 4313
Fax: (27) 563 4319

MALAYSIA

Outward Bound Trust of Malaysia
28th Floor; Menara Boustead
69 Jalan Raja Chulan
50200 Kuala Lumpur
Vice President: Tan Sri Dato' V. M. Hutson
Telephone: (60) 3 241 90 44
Fax: (60) 3 241 91 64

Outward Bound School Lumut
Teluk Batik
Lumut 32200, Dinding
Perak
Warden: V.A. Allan
Telephone: (60) 5 935077
Fax: (60) 5 935933

Outward Bound Trust of Sabah
Locked Bag 181
88745 Kota Kinabalu
Sabah
Chairman: Tengku Datuk Z Adlin

Outward Bound School Kinarut
Locked Bag 181
88745 Kota Kinabalu
Sabah
Warden/Director: Nick Cooke
Telephone: (60) 88 750311
Fax: (60) 88 750312

NETHERLANDS

Vormingscentrum Outward Bound
Annevillelaan 101
4851 CB Ulvenhout
Director: J. Holtrop
Telephone: (31) 76 612298
Fax: (31) 76 100118

NEW ZEALAND
Outward Bound Trust of New Zealand
P.O. Box 3158
Wellington
Exec. Director: Des Lyons
Telephone: (64) 4 723 440
Fax: (64) 4 728 059

Cobham Outward Bound School
Anakiwa, Private Bag
Picton
Director: Bruce Cardwell
Telephone: (64) 54 42016
Fax: (64) 57 42350

SINGAPORE
Outward Bound School
AFPN: 1263 Mindef General comcen
Singapore 2366
Warden: Major Lim Hong Kang
Telephone: (65) 5453548/5456707
Fax: (65) 5459008/5459005

TANZANIA
Outward Bound Centre
P.O. Box 95
Marangu
Contact: Aaron Chomolla
Telephone: Marangu 94

Outward Bound Tanzania
P.O. Box 4284
Dar es Salaam
Contact: Principal Secretary

UNITED KINGDOM
Outward Bound Trust
Chestnut Field, Regent Place
Rugby, Warwickshire CV21 2PJ
England
Chairman: Sir James Swaffield
Director: Ian L. Fothergill
Telephone: (44) 788 560423
Fax: (44) 788 541069
Outward Bound City Challenge
10 Rodney Street
Liverpool
Merseyside L1 2TE
England
Director: Jon Rigby
Telephone: (44) 51 707 0202
Fax: (44) 51 707 0711

Outward Bound Aberdovey
Aberdovey
Gwynedd LL35 0RA
Wales
Principal: Mike Pogodin
Warden: Dave Williams
Telephone: (44) 654 767464
Fax: (44) 654 767835

Outward Bound Rhowniar
Tywyn
Gwynedd LL36 9HT
Wales
Warden: Simon Waring
Telephone: (44) 654 710 521

Outward Bound Eskdale
Eskdale Green, Holmrook
Cumbria CA19 1TE
England
Principal: Bob Barton
Telephone: (44) 94 67 23 281
Fax: (44) 94 67 23 393

Outward Bound Ullswater
Ullswater
Penrith, Cumbria CA11 0JL
England
Principal: Steve Howe
Telephone: (44) 76 84 86347
Fax: (44) 76 84 86405

Outward Bound Loch Eil
Achdalieu, Fort William
Inverness-shire PH33 7NN
Scotland
Principal: Terry Small
Telephone: (44) 39 77 72866
Fax: (44) 39 77 72869

UNITED STATES OF AMERICA
Outward Bound U.S.A.
384 Field Point Road
Greenwich, CT 06830
President: John F. Raynolds III
Telephone: (1) 203 661 0797
Fax: (1) 203 661 0903

Colorado Outward Bound School
945 Pennsylvania Street
Denver, CO 80203-3198
Exec. Director: Mark Udall
Telephone: (1) 303 837 0880
Fax: (1) 303 831 6987
Hurricane Island Outward Bound School
P.O. Box 429,
Rockland, ME 04841
President: Stephen S. Kaagan
Telephone: (1) 207 594 5548
Fax: (1) 207 594 9425

North Carolina Outward Bound School
121 North Sterling Street
Morganton, NC 28655-3443
Exec. Director: John C. Huie
Telephone: (1) 704 437 6112
Fax: (1) 704 437 0094

Pacific Crest Outward Bound School
0110 SW Bancroft Street
Portland, OR 97201
Exec. Director: Paul D. Hart
Telephone: (1) 503 243 1993
Fax: (1) 503 274 7723

Voyageur Outward Bound School
10900 Cedar Lake Road
Minnetonka, MN 55343
Exec. Director: Nan Skelton
Telephone: (1) 612 542 9255
Fax: (1) 612 542 9620

New York City Outward Bound Center
140 West Street, Suite 2626
New York, NY 10007
Exec. Director: Richard Stopol
Telephone: (1) 212 608 8899
Fax: (1) 212 608 9250

ZAMBIA
Outward Bound Association of Zambia
P.O. Box 51004
Lusaka
Chairman: Rodgers Mumbi
Telephone: (260) 1 211619

Outward Bound Lake School
P.O. Box 420082
Mbala
Coordinating Secretary: Austin Mwanza
Telephone: (260) 4 450437

ZIMBABWE
Outward Bound Zimbabwe
Executive Council & Information/Postal Office
P.O. Box 1997
Harare
President: Denis L. Berens
Telephone: (263) 4 704461
Secretary: Mrs Barbara Makandanje

Outward Bound Zimbabwe Chimanimani Centre
P.O. Box 57
Chimanimani
Warden: Fenwick Goodes
Booking Secretary: Mrs Jacqui Goodes
Telephone: (263) 26 5440

Primary sources for the history of Outward Bound are an "Archival Statement" by Tom Price; *Outward Bound U.S.A.* by Joshua L. Miner and Joe Boldt; and research/compilation of a number of records by Liz Cole. Additional source material included *Inside Outward Bound* by Renate Wilson; *The Challenge of Outward Bound* by Basil Fletcher; *Outward Bound* by David James; *Outward Bound: Schools of the Possible* by Robert Godfrey; *Impelled into Experiences* by J.M. Hogan; Outward Bound International Newsletters nos. 1-9; and personal statements by Tom Price, Josh Miner, and Ian Fothergill.

The 32 Centre/School Reports are based on the work of scores of people from 18 countries on 5 continents who provided virtually all the information.

The quotes throughout this book represent reactions from students and staff from many of the Outward Bound schools around the world.

The statements on the topic "What Outward Bound Means to Me" are the words of Freddie Fuller, Garry Edward Richards, Derek Pritchard, John C. Huie, Tom Price, Ulf Handel, and Bob Pieh.

My personal thanks to Ian Fothergill and Liz Cole for their support, cooperation, and enthusiasm; to Richard Cohn and Cynthia Black for their encouragement and hospitality; and to Mark Zelinski for his photo captions and for his vision that led to this book.

PHOTOGRAPHER'S ACKNOWLEDGMENTS

This collection of photographs can give only a glimpse into the exceptional work that is being done by Outward Bound schools worldwide. To attempt more would demand a much larger book and a much longer schedule.

As early as 1984, Michael Waldin, an excellent designer, desktop publisher, and good friend, shared with me a vision of producing this book. Together we worked as partners on this project until 1989. His contribution to the work is immeasurable.

Many thanks to Doreen Gregson and Cynthia Long for their assistance in the writing of the photo captions and to Linda McKnight for all her counsel. Thanks also to Cynthia Black and Richard Cohn of Beyond Words Publishing, Inc. for bringing this book to fruition.

I would like to extend my appreciation to the sponsors, Sun Life of Canada and Canadian Asset Management, for their generous contributions toward the creation of this book, with special thanks to Linda Mackenzie at Sun Life. Thanks also go to Compass North Designs Ltd., Vancouver, for the use of their excellent outdoor clothing and equipment.

There are far too many deserving individuals from Outward Bound around the world to thank on this page. I am particularly grateful to John Greene (U.S.A.), Liz Cole (U.K. Trust), Ian Yolles (Canada), Derek and Pat Pritchard (Hong Kong), David and Emily Lam (Hong Kong), Ger Koekkoek (Netherlands), Scott Lee (Australia), Roger Binns (Lesotho), Lisa Garfinkle (Lesotho), Graeme Lamb (Aberdovey), Al Brown and family (Utah), and all at the Belgian Outward Bound School. Thanks to Ian Fothergill for permission to start this book and to Gary Shaeffer for writing the history and school reports. To all the Outward Bound staff who guided me through the wilderness, and occasionally to the pub, thank you.

Special thanks to the Gregsons on both sides of the Pacific, to Tony Iorio for his companionship in the American West, to Terri for giving me inspiration, to Nel for her encouragement, and to my brother, Matt.

Finally, thanks to Joe and Loraine, my parents, who gave me support and love through the hard times. Without their caring and strength, this book would not exist.